Erotic and Sexy Poems

Sensitive and Erotic poems

Michaela Iacoe

By Michaela Iacoe
Published: March, 24, 2014
Words: 13.827 (approximate)
Language: English
ISBN: 9798686608924

Adult Reading Material

I've learned that people will forget what you said, and people will forget what you did, but people will never forget how you made them feel.

And I will never forget how you made me feel.

Thank you very much my friend M H.

If you Need

If you want to tell me your secrets

I am all ears.

If your dreams do not work out,

I will always be there for you.

If you need to hide,

You will always have my hand.

Even if the sky crashing down,

I will always be with you.

Whenever you need a place,

There will be my song, you can get.

If someone breaks your heart,

Together we will take care.

When you feel emptiness,

You will not be alone.

If you get lost out there

I will seek you.

I'll take you somewhere

If you need to think

And when all seems to be lost,

And you need someone

I'm always here.

Secret of life

I understood that to live is to be free ... That you need to have friends ... that you need fighting to stay alive ... that to be happy, is just need you want to be happy ... I learned that time heals, That what hurts, goes ... That disappointment does not kill ... That today is a reflection of yesterday ... I realized that we can cry without shedding tears ... that true friends remains ... That a pain ... strengthens, that win magnifies ... I learned that dreaming is not fantasize ... that to smile you need to make someone smile ... that beauty is not what we see, but what we feel.

That the value is in the strength of achievement... I realized that words have power ... That to do is better than to talk ...That the eyes does not lie. That living is learning from mistakes. I learned that everything depends on the will. That the best is we be ourselves. That the SECRET of life is TO LIVE! "

And one of the things I learned is that one should live in spite of. Despite, one must eat. Despite, we must love. Despite, it must die. Even it is often the very despite that pushes us forward. It was despite that gave me an anguish that was unsatisfied creator of my own life.

Happiness

I do not know if life is short or long for us, but I know that nothing of what we have felt, does not make sense if not we touch people's hearts.

Often simply be: lap that welcomes, arm which involves, word that comforts, silent that respect, joy that is contagious, tears that flowing, look that caress, wish that satiates, love that promotes.

And this is not something from another world, is what gives meaning to life. That's what makes it is neither short nor too long, but it is intense, true, pure while it lasts. Happy is the one that transfers what you know and learn what you teach.

.

Pupil

I choose my friends not by skin or other archetype, but by the pupil.

Gotta have questioning shine and unsettled tone.

I'm not interested in the good spirits or bad habits.

I'm with those who make me crazy and blessed.

Of them do not want the answer, I want of them, my inside.

That they bring doubts and fears and to tolerate the worst in me.

For this only being crazy.

I want the saints so they do not doubt of differences and ask forgiveness for the injustices.

I choose my friends for the soul clean and by the face exposed.

I do not want only a shoulder and a lap, I also want his greatest joy.

A friend that does not laugh together, also don't know to cry together .

My friends are all like that, half foolish, half serious.

I do not want predictable laughs or cries merciful.

I want serious friends, those who make reality their source of learning, but that fight to keep fantasy alive.

I do not want adult or boring friends.

I want them half childhood and half old age!

Children, to not forget the value of the wind on their faces and old age so that have never hurry.

I have friends to know who I am.

Then seeing them crazy and saints, silly and serious, young and old, I never forget that normality is an illusion buster and sterile.

Friendship

Friendship

is the most beautiful affluent of love,

it helps solve

with patience,

the complicated equations

of human coexistence.

The friendship

is as strong as love,

it educates,

signaling the path of coherence

pointing out the paths of justice

controlling the excesses of passion.

The friendship

is a strong bond that unites people

in the chain of willing.

Friendship

IS glue divine,

too much glue,

can hurt.

The friendship

has much more

judgment that love,

when it exhausts

and schism to leave,

it purports to be

watching over

the feeling is left

Friendship

is the most beautiful affluent of love,

it helps solve

with patience,

the complicated equations

of human coexistence.

Friend

A friend is the result of a choice.

It is a choice of love

It is the discovery of the soul sister.

It is a clear awareness of something sublime and

permanent

that is not in the nature of things perishable.

It is a priceless treasure, like without distance,

someone present in our way,

in times of doubt, joy, too much to be lost,

important to be forgotten

My friends

I have friends who do not know how much they are my friends. Do not realize the love I devout to them and the absolute need that I have of them.

Friendship is a feeling nobler than love, behold, it allows the object to divide into other emotions while love has intrinsic jealousy, that does not admit the rivalry.

And I could bear, although not without pain, who had died all my loves, but would go crazy if die all my friends! Even those who do not realize how much they are my friends and my life depend on your existences...

Some of them do not seek, I just know they exist. This mere condition encourages me to move on with life.

But why not seek them assiduously, cannot tell them how much I love of them. They would not believe. Many of them are reading this chronicle and not know they are included in the sacred relationship of my friends.

But it is delicious that I know and feel that I admire them, love them, although not declare.

I need

I Need somebody
That looks me in the eye when I talk.
That hear my sorrows and neurosis with patience.
And that you do not understand yet, respect my feelings.
I need someone who will fight beside me without being convened;
Someone friend enough to tell me the truths I do not want to hear,
even knowing that I may hate him for it.
In this world of skeptics, I need someone that believes,
in this mysterious thing, discredited, almost impossible: Friendship.
That wrestle to be loyal, simple and fair, that does not go away if I ever
lose my gold and no longer be the sensation of the party.
I need a friend to receive with gratitude my help, my outstretched hand.
Even if this is too little for your needs.
I need a friend who is also a partner in binges and fishing, wars and joys, and through the storm, shout in chorus with me:
'We will still laugh a lot of it all', and laugh a lot.
I could not pick the ones that brought me into the world, but I can choose my Friends.
And in this quest commitment to my own soul because with a True Friendship,
life becomes simpler, richer and more beautiful.

If you are

If you are a winner,
will have some false friends
and some true friends.
Succeed anyway.

If you are honest and frank,
people may cheat you
Be honest and frank anyway.

What you spend years building
Someone could destroy overnight.
Build anyway.

If you find serenity and happiness,
People may be jealous.
Be happy anyway.

Give the world the best you have,
it may never be enough.
Give the best you've got anyway.

Friends

Friends are like the wind ...

It is impossible to hold them in my hands ...

They sometimes have other direction,

A path that is not our ...

Friends are like the wind ...

Sometimes "Hurricane", invading our lives ...

Sometimes "breeze", caressing our souls.

Friends are like wind ...

Sometimes close, sometimes far away ...

But forever in our hearts!

Miss you

When at night I cannot see you

Tell how was my day

Hearing your voice and fantasies

I miss the nagging boy

Who fought for a moment

A love without torment,

This love without suffering

Became our feeling

Our love

No limits, no rules in our love

surprising as rain in summer

appears without even we realize

Feel your breath is smelling flower field

Being useless is not believing

tomorrow, because love will increase

The wind changed my direction

I'm stuck

walking for shelter meeting

with the moon

No light following in the mist of lost way

in the absence of your affection

Embrace that naive woman who needs your affection

Let him lie in your arms

that look is lost in the crowd

Secure the black angel and says all will be fine

The power of friendship

The power of friendship overcomes all differences...
By the way...
What differences if we are friends?
When we make mistakes, we forgive and forget
If we have defects...
We do not care...
We exchanged secrets and we respect differences
Friend is no color, no gender, no age...
Friend is just a friend!
We admitted, we defended.
Without asking and we are always present
Not only in times of joy sharing pleasures,
But especially in difficult times
We make because we feel happy to make!
We are far and at once so near...
But what unites us can overcome all distances.
It is stronger than time, could cross
The immensity of space and transcend the limits of life.
Yes.. How strong it is because this feeling anything or anyone will destroy.
That it remains while our souls exist...
That neither the distance nor the time or even
Our mistakes, take to an end!
I love you my friend!

A platonic love.

One lives on the moon, the other anywhere in the space that is far enough not to be able to touch each other. Exchanged messages, one trembled at the sound of each other voice, sighing in dreams awake. Years dreaming of what would be the date of their lives, but that never happened. Maybe they were lost between one story and another, but always come back to look by far and with the same desire as always, because they have the same soul, just born in different places.

Small verse

In a small box, your look

Always will be saved

But at night is freed

And flies starry sky

And enters without ceremony

In dreams of lethargy

And in oneiric verses

Turns into poetry

If I was a poet

If I was a poet
could say in verse
All I feel for you
Would make our Relationship
meetings like magic
of angels singing in choir ...
If I were a poet
could mean _ rhymes,
I want you, love you and could ...
Unlock our fears
liberate our secrets,
let loose the thrill ...
With feelings of donation
delivery body and soul
representing the release.
Hugs smart,
bodies _ opened in
eagerness
Madness, sanity
mixed ...
As I am not a poet,
I can only tell you
love you, I want you
with much love and understanding.

Love and Passion

Passion is fire, lasting or passenger

that warms the chest, ignites and satisfies

Delirium of soul snatching the body and mind

But to hurt and hurt it is able

Love is breeze, fragrant, early morning

A rainbow on shades of tenderness

Safe haven, our essential lumen

Anchor and fount of pure happiness.

Walk the passion in a devastating action

And love, an everlasting enchantment

If the tornado of passion leaves us brands

The breeze of love relieves the suffering

To live happily

To live happily it takes a lot

little bit ...

An affectionate look ....

A handshake .... A smile ....

An long kiss ....

A joke soundly ...

Just the presence of someone

to everything else is just

happiness ...

Live each moment with love and

dignity. And in the future tell to

your children and grandchildren the secret to

live happy. Being a friend is all

that cares!

Friends are

Friends are for all life,

although they are not with us the whole life.

Friendship is not dependence and submission. You do not

have friends to agree in full, but to review the drafts and

doubt of the letter. It is independence, and respect.

What is most important: physical proximity or emotional?

As there are imaginary friends in our childhood, there are

invisible friends in our maturity. Those who do not are

close may be inside. Friend is what remains after the

hangover. It is glucose in blood. It is serenity.

How I want to be your friend

I want to be your friend. Not too much and not too little.

Not too far nor too close.

In the way as accurate as I can.

But love you without measure and stay in your life,

As discreetly as I know.

No take away your freedom, never suffocate you.

Without forcing your will.

Without speaking, when it's time to shut up.

And without silence, when it's time to talk.

Or absent, or present far too.

Simply, quietly, be your peace.

It's nice to be friends, but I confess it is so hard to learn!

And so I beg you, patience.

I will fill your face with memories,

Give me time to hit our distances ..

I need someone

I Need Someone
That looks me in the eye when I talk.
That hear my sorrows and neurosis with patience.
And that you do not understand yet, respect my feelings.
I need someone who will fight beside me without being convened;
Someone friend enough to tell me the truths I do not want to hear,
even knowing that I may hate him for it.
In this world of skeptics, I need someone that believes,
in this mysterious thing, discredited, almost impossible:
Friendship.
That wrestle to be loyal, simple and fair, that does not go away if I ever
lose my gold and no longer be the sensation of the party.
I need a friend to receive with gratitude my help, my outstretched hand.
Even if this is too little for your needs.
I need a friend who is also a partner in binges and fishing, wars and joys, and through the storm, shout in chorus with me:
'We will still laugh a lot of it all', and laugh a lot.
I could not pick the ones that brought me into the world, but I can choose my Friend.
And in this quest commitment to my own soul because with a True Friendship,
life becomes simpler, richer and more beautiful.

Friends are...

Friends are like the wind ...

It is impossible to hold them in my hands ...

They sometimes have other direction,

A path that is not our ...

Friends are like the wind ...

Sometimes "Hurricane", invading our lives ...

Sometimes "breeze", caressing our souls.

Friends are like wind ...

Sometimes close, sometimes far away ...

But forever in our hearts!

A friend

A friend is the result of a choice.

It is a choice of love

It is the discovery of the soul sister.

It is a clear awareness of something sublime and

permanent

that is not in the nature of things perishable.

It is a priceless treasure, like without distance,

someone present in our way,

in times of doubt, joy, too much to be lost,

important to be forgotten

Your look

In a small box, your look

Always will be saved

But at night is freed

And flies starry sky

And enters without ceremony

In dreams of lethargy

And in oneiric verses

Turns into poetry

Friendship

Confidence, like art, it has not derived the answer to everything, but to be open to all questions.

Pain nourishes courage. You cannot be brave if just happened wonderful things with you.

Hope is a loan application to happiness.

Happiness is not a prize, but rather a consequence, loneliness is not a punishment, but a result.

Happiness is not the end of the day, but at every turn that traveled to find it.

We always stumble on small stones, because the big ones we just see.

The glory of friendship is not the outstretched hand, nor the kindly smile, nor the delight of the company. It is the spiritual inspiration that comes when you discover that someone believes and trusts you.

True Friends

The misfortune has that good: it makes us aware of the true friends.

Intelligence is the beacon that guides us, but it is the way that makes us move.

The biggest weakness of a person is to change what he wants most in life, for what we want right now.

Persistence is the way to success.

The worst loneliness is one that sits in the company of others.

Solitude is a drop in the ocean that just look for itself.... A drop that doesn't know what is the ocean...

Friends are another part of the ocean looking for the drop...

Your only obligation throughout your existence is be true about yourself. True friendship leave positive marks that time can never erase. True friendship is one that asks nothing in return.

Real generosity is doing something good for someone else you'll never find out.

True freedom is all about power itself.

Some people find themselves educated because they compare their own ignorance with the others.

True friend is one who turns a small moment in a great while.

Friend is the light that doesn't leave dark the life.

A friend is one who knows all your secrets and still likes you!

A friend is one who makes us feel better about everything and makes us feel loved...

A friend is one who, every time, makes us understand and travels with us part of the way.

Friends are like flowers each one has its charm so cultivate them.

Friendship is like music: two strings tuned in the same tone, vibrating together.

Friendship (2)

Friendship, word for various feelings that cannot be changed by mere material things ... It should be kept and preserved into the heart!

People come into our lives by chance, but it is not accident that they remain.

Celebrate Life is to add friends, experiences and achievements, always giving them some meaning.

Friends Praise in public, criticize in private.

To err is human, to forgive is divine, so friends are divine.

Avoiding happiness for fear that it ends, it is the best way to be unhappy.

Make friends with the goodness of people, not with your goods!

Happiness is the certainty that our life is not going to no avail.

Thinking of you

Now I think of you

Look at the stars of the sky

I think most of you,

Not because the stars are similar

with the brightness of your eyes,

but because they are

so far from me ...

 I am writing

Just to know

What do you think

Of the verses that I did

Undo the wind

What's inside

of this place

That no one else stepped...

You are viewing

What is happening

In this booklet

I know they are still...

The verses

So yours that I ask

The verses

So mine that I expect

You accepted them...

Poets

I'm lost in those green dreams
Of being born and did not know who I am,
I walk a little blind girl groping walls
And I do not even know who blinded me!

I see nothing; everything is dead and vague...
And my soul blind, abandonment
Reminds me of a water lily from a lake
Extending the white wings of the dream...

Having within the soul, the light of the world
And I see nothing in this bottomless sea,
Poets my brothers, sad fate! ...
And others, they call us "the Illuminated"!
Poor blind blameless, sinless,
We suffer for the others until death!

Crazy heart

My crazy heart where are you going,

In your immense desire for freedom?

Take caution with reality;

My poor heart looks pier!

Let yourself be quiet! Don't love

The sweet stillness of solitude.

Your pretty unreal chimeras

Not worth the pleasure of a longing!

You call to my chest, black prison! ...

Ah, see well, Oh mad heart

Don't blot from yourself the shine of the moon!

Don't lay your wings to far...

Let yourself be quiet, sad monk

In the peace of your cell to sob! ...

[Erotic and Sexy Poems], por [Michaela Iacoe]

Me in sober colors

I am a child

Despite my forty-three years

Despite my many loves

One child ...

And I'm a little girl

A small, a weasel

Feathers larks

A little girl ...

My kids contest my maternal protests

But I defend myself

And keep a child

[46]

Passionate and at times

I throw myself to the torments

One child ...

My soul challenges the assurances of my skin

I dream now

Because I am a child

I turn back the time

Hair and skirt to the wind

One child....

You are

Even without seeing you

I even think I'm doing well

Just show up, so to speak

When I should appear

Or when I want

I design your face in my mind

I scribble the sun blotted out the rain

I want that you know I remember

I wanted you could see me

You're part of that makes me strong

And to be honest,

Very happy ...

Thinking of you (2)

I envision the walls of loneliness

and I walk among the sphinxes

of thought,

when the silent scream, stopped

cuts through the sound barrier

and the words crumble,

lost, empty themselves

cease to be to exist

when I meet them

in silence like calm

candor

of thinking of you...

When You Came Into My Life

You give me your smile

A piece of your heart

You give me the feel

I've been looking for

You give me your soul

Your innocent love

You are the one

I've been waiting for

I've been waiting for

We're lost in a kiss

A moment in time

Forever young

Just forever

Just forever in love

When you came into my life

It took my breath away

Cause your love, has found its way

Into my heart, Oh, yea

You make me dream

By the look in your eyes

You give me the feel

I've been longing for

Oh, I give you my soul

All my life

Cause you are the one

I've been waiting for

I've been waiting for, so long

When you came into my life

It took my breath away

And the world stopped turning round

For your love

When you came into my life

It took my breath away

Cause your love, has found its way

Into my heart

Into my heart

Just forever in love

When you came into my life

It took my breath away, oh yeah

And the world stopped turning round

For your love

When you came into my life

It took my breath away, oh yeah

Cause your love, has found its way

Into my heart

When you came into my life.

Don't Forget About Me

The swallows left

From my cold and sunless country,

Searching for Springs full of violets

And lovely and happy nests.

My little swallow left

Without leaving me a kiss

She left without a goodbye

Don't forget about me:

My life is tied to you

I love you more and more

In my dream you stay

Don't forget about me

My life is tied to you

There's always a nest

In my heart for you

Don't forget about me

You drag our life

Without a breathing moment

To dream

To be able to remember

What we have already lived

Without an end

You are a never ending moment

you have no yesterday

You have no tormorrow

Now everthing is in your hands

Large hands

never ending hands

I don't care about the moon

I don't care about the start

You for me are the moon and the stars

You for me are the sun and the sky

You for me are everything

All that i want to have

Never ending

Never ending

My sun

What a beautiful thing is a sunny day

the fresh air after the storm

from the fresh air the feast starts already

what a beautiful thing is a sunny day

But another prettier doesn't exist

my sun is your forehead!

Sun, my sun

is your forehead... is your forehead.

There's a light at the panes of your window

a laundress sings and boasts

and as she wrings, spreads and sings

there's a light at the panes of your window.

But another prettier doesn't exist

my sun is your forehead!

Sun, my sun

is your forehead... is your forehead.

When the night comes and the sun sets

almost a melancholy overcomes me

I would stay at your window

when the night comes and the sun sets

But another prettier doesn't exist

my sun is your forehead!

Sun, my sun

is your forehead... is your forehead.

How I love you

The wine is better in your mouth

I love you is gentler on your voice

The night in your body is shorter

I'm getting sick of love

Wish caress your hair

Wanted to be the night on your skin

Thinking it was all a dream

And then discover you again

And love you like I did,

How a woman loves a man

Have you as my only one

And not being able to believe

So mine that is part of my skin

Meet you was my luck

Loving you is a delight.

I wanted to drink from your chest

The honey of dawn

My fingers seeking for ways

Reaching the end of your skin,

Dance the Waltz of the waves

Body to body, you and I

I merge with you in the shadows

Making you a love poem

And love you like I did,

How a woman loves a man

Love, wine and rain

Night of Rain

Love in a cup, mixed with red wine

Kisses with grape flavor

Caresses that I drank

Body to body, soft ... Dry.

Bowls of warmth with red wine

Overflowing, releasing,

Emotions in small gulps,

Drunk us with desire.

Glass of madness mixed with the red wine,

Bodies wet with the rain that falls.

Devoting themselves fully, in ecstasy,

In the opium of foolishness ... Numbing

reason.

Glass with wine, forgotten, face,

Mute witnesses of the love that rests,

Balance the senses, reason...

Glass of calm ... In the wine ... with hope.

If we love each other

Ah, if we lose the notion of time

If we together have thrown all away

Tell me now how do I will stay ...

Oh, if since when I knew you

I live dreaming, I made so many follies

I broke with the world, burned my ships

Tell me where I can still go?

If we, in the follies of an eternal night

We confuse our legs

Tell me with what legs I must follow?

If we had spill our luck on the floor

If in the mess of my heart

I miss the vein and my blood ...

How if we love each other like two pagans

Your body is still in my hands

Tells me with what face I'll leave?

Moments

Moments are stored ...

some in the memories ...

but hidden ...

some with hope

others forgotten

Strong moments ...

Weak moments ...

Happy and sad sometimes

Times of meetings and ... of mismatches also

Moments of enjoy ... to fall in love ... and finally, to love

Ah .. moments of love

Magic moments

Moments when our eyes see more

Moments in which we see truly what is beautiful

Times when we find the best side of human ...

It is inside ...

Moments ... ah moments

Moments of listening,

Moments of talking

Moments to applaud ... to thank

Moments of madness ... of pleasure

Moments in which I wrote a poem for you

Moments only ours ...

Just me and you!

How you changed me

Tears, torments

How many disappointments

So many hardships and disappointments

But one day , destine changed everything

I met you and

My tears have dried

My torment ended

It was a cloud that passed

And now my life is a carousel of joy

And to top it off

I'm loving the fact

Forgive me if I outrank me in my euphoria

But is that now I know what happiness is

Rose

Red Rose,
Petal wet
its aroma and color
with a smell
due
fragrance of love.

Today it is scheduled,
it is the flower of love
illustrious in the land,
that lovely button
blooms
in the eyes
and in the heart
fluid Love
of eternal passion.

Rose in the ear

and chest

of woman awkwardly ...

that was beautiful!

Petal of Velvet

in lighted candle,

drop of water spilled,

in the bath balm

a crazy love.

Dry rose and beautiful

always comes back to land

tear immortalized

for whom so much ...

loved!

What goes on my mind

It has been a corner of joy

Muse than I write in its praise,

because that a blue veil of fantasy

about the impossible dream of love ...

It was light, it was sound, beauty and color

fleeting in my world each day,

it was after all: perfume and flower

a dull and empty life ...

What is this on my mind

as one in which the beach shuttle, or

a star shining in the sky ...

Was shooting star ... flashed

high in the heavens, a fleeting moment

and ... in the shadows of the night went off!

Jealous

Are you a jealous person? Suffers a lot from it? Indeed, jealousy moves a lot with us.

We are much attached to people we like to live, whether our children, spouses, parents, friends. It's great to have the illusion to think that we have something that makes us feel safe, believing that we have control of the people, they are ours as an object, I relate when I want, and the way I please. The fact is that we have nothing; we do not control anything in the same way that I can live with someone today; tomorrow I may not be able to have the opportunity to find that person again, either for whatever reason. So enjoy every day the chance to relate to people, like them or not, because they are an opportunity to become better beings.

Now, there is a difference when we talk about jealous of a friend, parent, brothers or sisters, compared people that we have a loving relationship or relationships that have sex and passion. This point more, polygamy is that we all have.

So do what, if we are polygamous beings! You cannot accept it, but every time you look at a person who calls your attention on the street, and has some desire in relation to it, you think this is what?

Okay, so what has to do with our polygamy, our jealousy? Ever heard that when we judge someone for something he did, in fact we are pointing on him something we need to improve in us? There is a phrase that Freud talks like "When Peter tells me about Paul, I know more about Peter than about Paul." So when we have the feeling of jealousy, that someone can do something with me, generating insecurity linked to treachery, the truth is that we would like to be with this possibility in our hands, but as someone cheating is wrong, and I cannot take this my will, I have just projecting on the partner something I want to do, but I cannot assume. In psychoanalysis this is called transfer by projection.

Ever I say this: assume your wills, without repression, but use your reason for coming to a conclusion, if it is compensated or not, doing what you're thinking. We need to be more rational, and let our emotions run free within four walls, with the person you choose to love, to have sex.

Next time when you're jealous, pay attention to how much you really do not like to be in his or her place, with the knife and cheese in hand, to do what so much accuses the other "possibly doing" (in your head) .

My beloved Friend

I remember you and our times

That can be compared to centuries

From an understanding, affection and dedication,

Love for each other, it is always so.

It always does.

Those who pass even realize that we are in an environment

Created by us, for us.

Where it does not fit the folly

Which leads to the failure of the human soul.

We are guided simply,

No wonder it is the happiness of every day.

I am happy to see you happy,

Take your pain as if it were mine alone.

I want to see you happy forever,

The smiling and singing through the clouds

That danced in the air.

Always with you

For better or worse

My Beloved Friend.

Do not expect this wickedness

Touch your heart,

Because my heart is always at your side.

I want to stay in your arms always welcoming.

I love you.

I want you so.

The difficulties of life do not come

If you think that will not come,

I want love, I want to learn to say:

Love you.

Dream of me

Dream of me, conquer the space that I offer

In your lonely nights looking into the heart

Your sleep will be light and quiet ... Dream of me

In your dream will give you everything you want in this

life

Loves impossible to win

Sincere and loyal friends always listen to you

The nostalgia will no longer feel,

The joy of feeling all around you to love

The happiness of having a full life in this plan

The achievement of all objectives as expected

Only have a feeling that I cannot offer

It is the feeling of hatred, because it cannot be acquired

It makes suffer and i do not want you to suffer

It brings unhappiness and want to see you happy

So just win the good feelings in this dream

Tonight forget everything and just dream...

Dream of me ... I'm your angel that makes you dream.

Where did I go wrong?

I was pleased to have you as a friend

But wonder what happened to me?

Where did I go wrong?

Sometimes I wonder if I do not get it wrong

Friendship with being in love

If it is only that, will soon pass

But when I see my messages I think: will be you?

What I am doing, I stop doing

And if you get too long without writing me

I look for an excuse to write to you

What a fool, but I cannot help myself

Because I live only thinking of you

And is unintentionally

You do not get out of my head anymore

And I live only awake to dream

Imagining we both

Sometimes I think it is an impossible dream, a terrible

illusion

Is it?

With you I am well

I'm thinking of you

Thinking of never

Think of forget you

Because when I think of you

It is only when I do not feel alone

With my poems and thoughts

With the scent of morning

With rain summers

With the design of apples

With you I am well.

Dreamed about you

I dreamed about you all night long

Light of my eyes, my heaven of stars

It was so lovely to spend the night with you

You told me I was a good angel

You surrendered to pleasure

Temptation that make you mine

Too bad there was just a dream

I woke up and you were not here

I'm feeling sad and alone

I need you to smile.

Do not want to wake up

Inspiration of my dreams, do not wanna wake up

I want to be alone with you; I will not be able to fly

To stop and reflect, if my reflection is you.

Learning one life, sharing the pleasure

Why it seems that time I will not hold,

If I ever have the strength, and never stopped fighting?

As a film, in the end everything will work out

Who said you need to stay close, to stay together?

Think of me, I'm thinking of you

And tell me, what I want to tell you

Dreaming of you

Late at night when all the world is sleeping

I stay up and think of you and I wish on a star

That somewhere you are thinking of me too

Because I'm dreaming of you tonight

Until tomorrow I'll be holding you tight

And there's nowhere in the world I'd rather be

Than here in my room dreaming about you and me

Wonder if you ever see me and I wonder if you

Know I'm there (Am I there)

If you looked in my eyes would you see what's inside

Would you even care

I just wanna hold you close but so far

All I have are dreams of you

So I wait for the day and the courage to say

How much I like you

Yes I do

I'll be dreaming of you tonight

Until tomorrow I'll be holding you tight

And there's nowhere in the world I'd rather be

Than here in my room dreaming about you and me

I can't stop dreaming of you.

About my love for you

Tonight I'll say about my love for you

It seems the natural thing to do

Tonight no one is gonna find us

We'll leave the world behind us

And I hope that deep inside you feel it too

Tonight our spirits will be climbing

To the sky lit up with diamonds

And soon this old world will seem brand new

Tonight we will both discover

How friends turn into lovers

Tonight there'll be no distance between us

What I want most to do

Is to get close to you

Will you still love me tomorrow?

Tonight, you`re mine completely, you give your love so
sweetly

Tonight, the light of love is in your eyes...

Will you still love me tomorrow?

Tonight with words unspoken, you said that I`m the only
one

But will my heart be broken, when the night meets the
morning sun.

Will you still love me tomorrow?

How I am

I am a dreamer and fickle stubbornly realistic. I have a sweet quiet living with my eternal anger. I'm completely lucid with my crazy moments. I am fully determined, but sometimes I'm not sure about this. I have an incredible intelligence that surpasses all my difficulties. I have an excellent memory to remember only what is convenient to remember. Sour taste, but I cannot resist the bitter. Suffer intensely but overcome later. Love and hate. Crying at the same time I find grace. I am a great friend but I'm selfish (when necessary). I am a woman who likes to be alone without being anti -social. I am a person who thinks for itself but considering the opinion of others in some situations. I am selective and somewhat friendly. I am against injustice but do not want to be a lawyer. I criticize but do not judge anyone. I am music and listener. I am a reader and writer. I am the antithesis. I am a verb. I have several hyperboles. I love irony. I am a noun with several adjectives. I'm not a language. I'm human.

Feel my embrace

Close your eyes and feel my embrace ... Just feel ...

My heart is looking for yours ...

In the silence of the night ...

I seek you in every thought ...

I pass my hours just dreaming ...

Mad desire to hug you ...

I know who you are to me

I make friendship by affinity, when I'm dating I have intimacy and I only get married for love and eternity. To me there is nothing more meaningful in life than this "everything".

My intimacies are not only linked to sex or nakedness, because being inside someone's chest and have someone else living in your thinking is to be connected by affection and divided by time, together or even distant. There is always something reminding me of you with great constancy.

When the laws of physics allow us to be living in the same place and the same time, the conversations will go through dawn, or if words fail us, look at the horizon in the same direction is enough. Our eyes are different, but we have the same look.

In the impossibility of touch, I can see you through the wind that comes through the window and the dreams I have of you is intimacy with you. It is penetrate your barriers, go to your deeper and find out what is inside your heart. Know of your light and know your shadow.

It is much more than overthrow the modesties, is an alchemy of two lives who met and that know each other. Many people who we do not know very well seem to be interesting .But the best of meet someone is that how much more we dive more we want to be sunken in them. Unlike the ordinary course of relationships, "the more I know and talk with you, more I love you."

Affinity

The affinity is not the brightest, but the most subtle and delicate of feelings. And it is also the most independent. No matter the time, the distances, when there is affinity, any meeting starts the relationship again, at the exact point where it was interrupted.

To have affinity is very rare. But when there is, no need to verbal code to manifest.

Existed prior knowledge, exist during and remains after that people are no longer together.

What you have difficulty expressing to a non-affine goes out simple and clear with someone with whom you have an affinity.

Affinity is like getting away thinking about the same facts that impress, touch or mobilize.

It's just talking, without exchanging words.

It is get what is coming from the acceptance previously of understanding...

Affinity is felt with. Not feeling against, or feel for.

To feel with, is no need to explain what you're feeling.

It is look and sees.

It's more silence than talk, or when speaking, never explain, just say.

Affinity is never feel for.

Who feels for, confuses affinity with masochism.

But to those who feel with, they evaluate without contaminating.

They understand without taking the other's place.

They accept for have the permission of questioning.

Who does not have affinity, questions for not accepting.

Affinity is resuming the relationship where you left off without regretting the time of separation. Because time and separation never existed.

Were only opportunities given (taken) for life, in order for the common maturation could take place.

And so every person could and can be increasingly the expression of the other in the magnified form of individual self-enhanced.

Feel Embraced

The average length of a hug between two people is 3 seconds. But the researchers found something fantastic. When a hug lasts 20 seconds, there is a therapeutic effect on the body and mind. The reason is that a sincere hug produces a hormone called "oxytocin", also known as the love hormone. This substance has many benefits in our physical and mental health, helps us, among other things, to relax, to feel safe and calm our fears and anxiety. This wonderful calming is offered free of charge every time we have a person in our arms. So my dear, feel my deep hug in you with the wind embracing your body.

My writings

Amongst all of my possible identities based on my race or class, gender or religion, profession or culture, the one that is closest to my heart is that of a writer. It is unique to me, reflecting my creative personality and my authentic self. When I am inspired and I pick up my pen, I feel connected to my most honest and intimate self. That is where all my affection and love resides. That is why I call my writings my love letters to humanity.

All my life I had an a concern reflected in my poem:

Understanding

Self-knowledge

Reflection

Love

The music inside

I feel fortunate that my inner music is still alive, expressing my creative self. My writings are reflections of my dreams, dreams of inner peace and a just and a peaceful world. I feel so fortunate that life gave me a gift of creativity and I enjoy sharing that gift with you and with all humanity.

When I reflect on my life as a writer I can see all the way back to my childhood. I was very fond of story books and loved to read them in my spare time. I was lucky that my dad regularly borrowed books from the school library. I might have inherited my love for books from my dad. I felt proud when I wrote my first poem.

I started writing regularly as a teenager when I was in pharmacy school. I used to entertain my class fellows with my poems and their appreciation inspired me to write more. As time passed I became serious about my writings and developed my identity as a writer. That identity strengthened when I became the editor of a magazine in the university.

Being a writer always made me feel special. I realized that I had a special gift that others lacked. When I became a short story writer I started challenging the hypocrisies of my social and cultural environment. I wanted to lead an honest life and be in touch with my truth and share it with others with my creative writing hoping that it would inspire others to get in touch with their truth and not be embarrassed about it. My writings helped me remain honest with myself. It was like my own self-therapy.

I find it interesting that of all the languages I learnt Portuguese, Italian English and French as a child, the one that attracted me the most was English as a medium of my creative expression. I used to go to local libraries and borrow books from the sections of poetry, fiction, psychology, religion and philosophy. I must have read hundreds of books as a teenager. Those were the years I was fascinated with:

...poetry of Fernando Pessoa

... theatre of William Shakespeare

....fiction of Thomaz Mann

...philosophy of Socrates and Plato

...politics of Marx and Lenin

...theology of Priest Antonio Vieira

and

...psychology of Freud and Jung.

It was strange that I felt more connected with the dead writers than living people all around me. That was the time I felt I was a member of a Writer's Club, a club that only existed in my mind.

After entering pharmacy school, I got deeply involved in chemical and immunology and had less time for my creative writings. But after my graduation from UNESP I came back to my creative poems, chronic and essays. But I realized that I had changed as a writer.

I had started writing professional essays in English rather than poems in Portuguese. Gradually my comfort and confidence in English increased and I started writing poems and stories directly in English. In the last decade I am realizing that there has been another metamorphosis in me as a writer.

A, After my book The beauty of Poetry was published and I was interviewed on a local journal, I started write more and more.

B, After starting my job and developing new ways of work relationship, I also started writing as a diary activity.

C, After I was invited to write regularly for a column for an internet website https://clubedeautores.com.br/ I have written on the subjects of friendship, love and some chronic in the last few years.

It seems as if the writer in me has been expressing himself as a poet and a critic. English seems the preferred medium. I want to write in a language and style that a grade ten person can read and understand as I want to share my ideas not to impress readers. I am a great admirer of folklore that is simple and profound and full of wisdom. That is why it is remembered and cherished by the masses rather than a few academics.

My hope is that my writings will decrease human suffering and increase quality of life of others.

I am neither a politician nor a political activist, I am a writer. But I believe that writers can play a significant role in creating social changes. They can inspire people to challenge oppressive systems and dream of a better future. They can bring an inner change and prepare people for social and political changes. Writers can play a role in human liberation and give people the courage to be free, emotionally as well as socially, politically as well as culturally. The way other writers' books helped me in liberating myself and getting in touch with my truth, I hope that my books will help others to get in touch with their truth and inspire them to creativity. I want to be a part of human evolution. I get great pleasure with the idea that those books will stay even after me death. It is my humble attempt to serve humanity and I hope my books can keep on serving humanity when I am not around. It is my creative link with my own and future generations. One evening in my diary I wrote.

I'd like to know

I wanted so much to know why I am I!
Who has rejected me in this dark path?
I wanted so much to know why I hold
In my hands the good that is not mine!

Who will tell me if, overhead, the sky
It is also for the bad, for the perjurer?
Where goes the soul that died?
I wanted to find God! So much, I look for Him!

The road to Damascus, my way
The star of my sky blind woman,
Water of the source that I'm thirsty!
Who knows if this desire for Eternity
stumbling in the shade, is in the Truth
It is already the hand of God who cherishes me?

Now I want thank you for giving me the inspiration to
write new poems.

Thinking of you

Ah, if only I could see you, and in my eyes you could look ... Perhaps then so you could understand how hard it is to love you.

If my hands touch you...

If I could kiss your lips ... So then I would know what flavor in them!

If I knew which songs you enjoys listening, for you I'd do a soundtrack to remember ... If I could remember ... Remember only that place.

Where for the first time my eyes met yours.

Maybe then be able to settle my thoughts ... And in that place, that place I could find you again.

From you never, never would separate me.

But like this is not possible, I continue to dream and wait for you.

Forbidden Love

Only those who lived understands

Forbidden love.

Move with the essence of the people,

With libido.

Everything is more exciting.

At the meeting hidden

The heart beats,

The face blush.

There are no those who support

The thrill of the first time

It's more excitement.

Mixture of fear and passion

Never regret.

The feelings leap to the eye,

The words are interspersed.

It seems that the whole world

Will discover that sin.

But with so much love,

Surely we will be forgiven

Seduction

Crimson lips

Wet

You fall on your knees

drops the thin sweater perfumed

heady

like nectar

more without ...

Seduce me!

abuses,

smears all

with him heaving wet

with milk and honey Roman

with words and defects.

mundane,

Human ...

Seduce me!

Fondly.

Delicate porcelain.

I wrap and I fool you

There is malice in the air.

Will flooding back

to us ...

but not yet!

Seduce you!

His eyes are no longer on me.

Are closed, guessing

my touches.

My sweaty hands

Leading you ...

... learn your body.

Seduce you!

each hair

every pore,

every square millimeter

this swarthy complexion

beg for me

And suddenly you sink

Repairs, then

that at the bottom and at the end

no more seduces ...

Seduced you confuse yourself,

with me.

The slide

slide

Your image on my mind

Your smell for my blood

Your voice, your words by my desire

slide

My hands through your hair

My mouth by your lips

My body for yours

slide

All that can have in the world

And however that's just us two

dancing like dream images

Slide dreams

endless spaces

Loves, uncontrollable passions

infinite

slide

Trembling nervously by my desire

Not to let you slide

Among my hands

Pleasure

Seek the Lord thy desire in my body crazy,
I'm a woman, I'm not a saint and to you I open my robe
if you drink in the morning mist the pleasure that is not little,
I'll lay my body in your bed causing you wonder.

In dismay, even away from the legacy way,
make my body your house to stay as fever,
languid in my skin with your delusions I lie
beautiful and pleasing I warmth you pulsing in my chest.

I am your sin be not tenderness,
get your wants in bed as your best creature
and sin .. very, by pleased not lose candor.

Make of skin, music as carving drunk
and of the poem a loose river toward the raging sea,
release the helm of the schooner, wrecked in the waves of
that gorgeous date.

Perfect fit

Every time I come to dream of you,
I wake up sweaty with pleasure.
I just cannot forget once.
The sweet love you give me
It's enough to get me involved with you.
Increasingly.

Just do not make me forget your perfume.
Neither your kiss too striking.
This strong passion that unites us.
It is the desire to satisfy me.
I close my eyes and see your face.
I feel your body on mine.
As the nail and the meat.
It's you and me.

As the gathering of wine and a glass.
Perfect fit, exact measurement.
So your kiss intoxicating.
Made me a slave of your love..

I wish you

I'm thinking of you,

and I wish you happiness.

And tomorrow, it will be the next day,

I still will wish you happiness.

I may not be able to tell you about it every day,

Because I might be absent, or we may be too busy.

But it makes no difference

- My thoughts and my wishes will be with you the same

way.

Any joy or success you have,

will make me happy.

I wish you all the happiness in the world.

Perfect Lover

I do not know how much time passed

before I succumb

but one day, it happened.

Succumbed to your charms.

And I surrendered.

It was a summer morning

I lay with you in the sand

seaside - shamelessly.

In the background,

percussion wave,

the gale,

treble extremes

Seagulls voyeurs.

You entered my womb,

my torso, my face, my plexus ...

My body was burning, without fever.

My sweat and my salt dripped,

no dramas.

And I dewatering right there

the foam of the waves ...

But you were insatiable

and followed invading me.

Hours passed

in which I have left

unhurried.

And when, finally,

looked at you confessing weariness,

excess heat and thirst

you gave me, gentleman,

with gentle raindrops.

Few loves

we wash the body and the soul ...

Only left me smile

enchanted.

Crazy love

I do not know if we are crazy

Or if our love was

Making us crazy.

Without knowing explain

This unbridled passion

We know that we are loved and passionate

I for you and you for me.

We so love our love

Became crazy and bold

But for us, wonderful!!

Love in Poetry

Destiny brought you to me

As the tide brings a seashell

As the wave breaks on the beach

You broke me.

There is no more to do

It was written to meet you

I loved you before you were born

And even after I die I will still love.

Everything that exists in the world of good

Everything that makes you smile

Makes me music and tone

Makes our melody exist.

A rhyme for you

In rhyming verse, stolen kisses

Cards stored, dusty dreams

Hugs, smiles wide open

Hands clasped, renewed promises

Have I ever told you that I love you without rhyme?

It's hardly a poet, wants to impress

I dream with you

What I feel is so simple and so crazy,

I dream with you.

I live

Unable to forget.

I'm feeling the longing to approach,

My eyes want to find you.

Cause I'm so alone,

Please tell me if you still want me.

Why am I so alone...

Please tell me if you still

Still want me.

What I feel is so simple and so crazy,

I dream with you.

The nights are empty because

I'm feeling the longing to approach...

Dreamed of you

Yesterday I dreamed of you, a dream that brought me memories unlived. And I began to remember that time we were together ... My heart raced, my mind would not let go you ... So I tried to close my eyes and sleep again, but when I closed my eyes, I saw you. I remembered then that it was lack of you, and longing was uncontrollable. I decided to get out of bed. I did everything I had to do, and waited for the right time to see you again ... - The right time? I was taking some time to see if all that feeling could disappear. And not disappeared ...

I went online, I saw and reviewed your photos, imagining you here. And then a sadness took my heart: View your photos was the only way to have you.

Other people want this feeling that was sudden to you, and sometimes I think : Is it possible or true? But I cannot deal with it, this feeling is reserved only for you, sometimes I think it was always so. Since an attraction like this is very rare.

I do not know how long this will last, I do not know how long we wait, I just want it to happen how it should be.

Intercourse

nightfall

All gone

It's just me and you

In a universe only ours

at bedtime

I feel your breath on my face

My hands wander over your body

Your mouth approaching of my

with desire

with love

with affection

with heat

without words

only gestures

Nothing more is needed

When two bodies are joined

It's instinct

One comprises the other

Discovering what is promoted in other instants

Hands intertwine

Mouths breathing each other

Exhaling what they feel

Sweatin 'wishes

breathing horny

whispering moans

Until you reach the top

What was alive

Die briefly

The most erotic and intense feeling

Of love, lust

They want each other

For something which vitiates

And minutes later

The ritual begins

Love Ritual

Provoke me.

Quench my thirst.

Dominate me.

Throw me in your network.

Undo the ties.

Release the buttons.

Wrap me in your arms.

Vibrate my hamstrings.

Kiss my hair.

Bite my mouth.

Let me bite you

And rip your clothes off.

Touch me.

Quench my libido.

Kiss Me.

Rip my dress.

Crumble the qualms.

Loosen your desires.

Wrap me in your tempting lips.

Thrill to my kisses.

Kiss my navel.

Bite my neck.

Lie with me.

And start up my taste.

Kiss me.

Satisfy your hunger.

Fill me.

Scream my name.

Insatiable appetite

I have a own form of love

One way only mine

Sweet, sensual, engaging

My love is gentle but can become voracious

Depending on each time

It modifies ...

And an insatiable appetite

I'll make you my prey ...

Come, taste with relish

Feel like I am now, for you

Penetrate my being ...

Discover my charms

And all I can do ...

Enjoy every moment

Feel that yummy movement

Bodies who love each other wildly

Writhing in every way

And feeling the ecstasy comes, slowly ...

Feel the scent that exudes from my body

At this moment ...

The odor of love ...

Now, do not think

Just feel ...

Takes advantage, of this girl ...

A woman child, that I am

To make you happy in my bed

Of all the ways you think

And a universe of things to enjoy ...

Now, once again, comes ...

Come love me ...

LOVE ME FEARLESS

Imagine yourself in me,

safely in my arms!! Your hugs.

Swipe with your eyes over my body.

Loose!! Half naked ... I'm the Gypsy

both flames in poetry!! Our ties.

I'm insane in my desires.

Wait! My smell!! I want to give you.

remade my ways in ballads.

Outlines my breasts and kissing without fear.

I look for you by my poem.

Come on! As a king! In seconds.

Relieves my secret with your tongue

makes me delirious in your fragrance,

I want you _ .

touches me with your deep movement.

My craving for pleasure!! Fill me,

by the taste of the mysteries that are in us.

Savoring me like nectar!! My sex.

Penetrate your gesture!! Enter in my sex

and do not be surprised if I come.

Explore!! Violate!! Do not ignore me,

I do not belong to you now in this time,

but I desire you!! Your desires without fear.

water me and delegate all your charm on me

and squeeze me in you ...

If you could

If you could for one instant being in me...

You would realize how much I want you

That in every smile

Hidden behind the screen

There is a heat of pleasure

An anxiety to love

Wanting to have a caring

A soul singing

If you could... for a moment

Being in me... would realize how much

I belong to you... Only for you

My heart opens... Even in the cold

Warms me... in the silence... I feel you

In the words... I welcome you

Your kisses... My wishes

If you could briefly be in me

Carrying me in space

Being in the constancy of time

Welcoming me into your arms

Loving you tirelessly

Handing me in

Your kneading

Feel in my body

And even though I do not want, you induce me
playing your game.

Numbs my senses, smothers my
moans, until provoke my enjoyment.

What power is this?
What wanton seduction, this is what I always feel
when you hold me?

Just see you online give chills in my skin, in
thermal shocks.
And I surrender peaceful, to your hypothetical desires .

Excite me and shocks me your boldness.
But when more and more, like growing up,
I embark on your fantasy.

And when delivered to our daydreams feeling in my body
yours swaying, nothing else matters.

Feel in my body (2)

I feel your tongue in my body.
That burns me
Like a fire whip.

And even though I do not want, you induce me
playing your game.

Numbs my senses, smothers my
moans, until provoke my enjoyment.

What power is this?
What wanton seduction, this is what I always feel
when you hold me?

Just see you online give chills in my skin, in
thermal shocks.
And I surrender peaceful, to your hypothetical desires .

Excite me and shocks me your boldness.
But when more and more, like growing up,
I embark on your fantasy.

And when delivered to our daydreams feeling in my body
yours swaying, nothing else matters.

You do not go out of my mind

I want you in my world,
even for just one second
wonderful to be at your side
and tell everybody that I'm your girlfriend
How and good be able to hold you
kiss your mouth and then love you
With you I lose my breath
I really find the owner of my heart
how this could have happened
if I even spoke that love needs a long time to happen
And you do not go out of my mind,
and it was so weird but I'm losing
for you, you can believe, then let it happen,
Love me the way I love you
Stop, Think and listen please
I really love you,
believe in my love
You was and is the most special
person in my life.

Yesterday I dreamed about you.

"When I walked into my room, there you were, sitting on my bed holding a huge poster. You ordered me to read every poster frame. The first square, said you had another one, as soon as I read looked at you, and you told me to continue. The second square was one of my texts. The third square, was a work of your college. The fourth square, spoke something about me that made me confused, but then, you put the finger on a small square , and there was a drawing of a heart, you smiled and said: "My heart is yours", then read what was written and I hear the words :

I said I did not want to, but it is becoming inevitable be in love with you. You barely gone, and I already miss you . - your presence is warm and pure, to be with you is to smile of life, is to find peace and forget the rest. Hearing your voice reassures me. Smell you, fills me with passion. See your smile ... Ah! Your smile! Touching your skin, to stroke your hairs, hug you! Our moments. that are ours alone, and each one better than the other, when they go they make me so ... Without peace.

Because things between us are really abstract. I do not know what you feel; you do not really know what I feel. But our moments speak for us. Has no duration, or warning that will last ... It just happens. There are not people in favor, nor people against - we follow our desires. Whenever one of us will be the wiser, and the other crazy, and then things are reversed. Will always have something to comment on, and things to be left in silence ... A look, or a kiss.

This is called affinity, and it exists even far away. Because you will be there, and I'll be here wondering. - How the starlight. - And I did not want to, but it is becoming inevitable. Just do not forget to come back because I do not forget to wait.

Desire to love

How to retain and suffocate

Inside the chest, at birth

Each cry of joy and pleasure

And the burning desire to love you?

Wanted to block this flame

That consumes me, which makes endless my nights

ah, how to understand this passion...

so far from you, without being able to hear that you love

me

When I wake up, away from you

I am depressed, lost around there

As a wandering being.

Dream to hear of your sexy voice

The invitation to glue our bodies and mouths

Delivering us to love as two passionate lovers

Whispers and spasms

Feel and desire, night and day, and your caresses and
kisses, look, your eyes .
Hear your voice whispering in my ear "I love you".

My hands are not my hands.
They are your body burning.

You, taste, smell, touch.
Heat.

Softness that runs every inch of my skin
While you sip your first wish of honey
With my tongue lost in the jungle of your privacy.

Fortress that does not hurt. Slowly, very slowly
caresses my whole skin. Gets to the top
of my desperate desire ... Soak up
of me to impregnate me of you ...

.

Ahhhhhhhh!!

Tangled up in me without looking at me or smile
And my face gradually becomes
From the usual expression to transfigure
In reincarnation of sublime ecstasy.

.

And more, more ... more ... well ... yeah ... yeah ... my
love.

More!
Thousand times trembling with cracklings
- Delivery of pleasure and anxiety as in a dream-
Magnetized our bodies do not separate ... not. No.

.

Tighter ... preached to me −

So!!, So ... Ahhhhh, Ahhhhh, Ahhhhh!!
...
Orgasms intertwined like a raging volcano
in spasms as the ground writhing - Aphrodite and Eros -
snap my moans and yours in unison.

.

Birth a new song of sounds inexpressible.
New words mixed with our kisses.
Delights crazed, hungry, thirsty.

.

Jungles!

Amazon jungle. Go through without bleeding,
feverish of pleasure-your name is an echo incessant
that seduces and provokes more-endless desires
insatiable,
between the valleys of my body you're reborn. Ridge
which rises
reborn as spring rebelling against the snow. Flourishes.

Templation

Do not tempt me, Oh boy,
With this divine beauty
That shows me almost naked ...
Do not tempt me, I freak out,
And forget the purity,
That you hint me ...

There are times that the desire
Crazy dream with your kiss,
Your mouth seduction ...
And now I see you thus
Projecting over me,
With so much provocation ...

If you try me, desirous,
How a cat sly,
With such audacity,
I'll throw you on the grass
And how the beasts in the jungle,
Possess you at once!

Cadence

Your breath saucy

Slide down the back of my neck

Dripped between my wanting

And your urgency plunges me.

My body is flame that your verb feeds

And that your breath nude, dress me

governing my symphony

Notes unhurried.

Your calculation is accurate

Wise and generous

And I bathe in your river

That wash up from my bowels of the heat.

Sex is sacred ...

Sex is sacred

as salty are the drops of sweat

that burst from my pores

drench our skins.

The night is my temple

where I become a goddess maddened

Feeling your hair on my skin.

Right now I am anything

body only,

mouth

skin

hairs,

tongues,

mouths.

And the life birth from the seed,

of the few seconds of ecstasy.

Your hands as a toy

wandering through my body.

Not reveal secrets

reveal only the shame of the world,

Discover the fever of animals.

Then we have become one

at the same time that

the darkness explodes in celebration.

The evening dawns without verses,

with the music of your breath gasping.

The sun arises from inside me.

Few seconds.

For a few moments spoil me of suffering.

I was happy.

Let's make a deal tonight

Let's make a deal tonight ... we're not so realistic.

You groans and sighs, I hear

while I explore you like crazy

floating in moons surrealists.

Let's make a deal tonight ... ephemeral is this flesh that seals us.

Time stops while you undress.

The world falls apart when you dress.

Love me before that the modesty tear you like a knife.

Let's make a deal tonight ... tears are crystals of the heart.

I feel the bile in your lips immaculate.

I see the abyss of your eyes masked

who hide behind of vain torments ...

Let's make a deal tonight ... no point escape from life itself!

Still fears the flower because of thorns.

Still believes that we will finish alone.

And love is no more than a lie.

Let's make a deal tonight ... promise to convince you in the stillness

that ideal love is to defoliate the days

happiness clouding our hatred

and I can always have this virtue.

Desire

I want to massage your body,

As if I serve you a tribute of passion.

And with my hands, as in a ritual,

Go through all your ways

And of it extract the flame of combustion.

And smell it entirely,

In the heat of sniff the core of your soul.

And kiss you voluptuously and with my lips

Absorb the crazed sweat of your pores

I want then joined bodies,

Dance at the sound of your moans and whispers

Dance smooth and amazing of love.

Love, Passion, Desire

We hugged affectionately,

giving ourselves to this love almost demented ...

Only your sweet smells I felt ...

In the union of our electric bodies,

uncontrolled, frenzied sensually,

plunged into complete dementia.

you groping my breasts ...

Our legs intertwined,

desire in our bodies hallucinated,

feeling the pleasure approximating

dominated by this crazy emotion ...

Unaware of what goes around,

our pleasure surpasses all limits ...

Your naked body is an eye candy for me ....

Touching you is a constant delight ...

I just want to love you again and again ...

Merge our bodies, perhaps

After overflowing of this sweet sensation,

I kiss your whole body with full devotion ...

Kiss your sex with affection and love ...

While my lips surrounding your cock,

everything around us gets another colorful ...

While we groan of intense pleasure and delight,

you want the warmth of your sex I enjoy ...

We give ourselves to our love impatient,

to this almost insane desire ...

With passion, our energy is renewed,

And our sexes more and more taste themselves,

in this our passion crazed,

that more times will be renewed ...

Tonight I need to love you

Today I came back because I missed you

I went back to kill the will

That is too much to talk to you

Let me touch your body in bed

To see you say you love me

Let, let me dream of you

Let me make your arms my nest

Tonight I need to love you

I want to have you by my side tonight

And live the moments dreamed

Tonight I need to love you.

COME TO ME ...

Come to me my love, make me happy,
come give me all your love kills me with pleasure ...
Ah! I'm completely crazy
when you start talking to me in the ear ..
I love exploring your body, love to take off your mouth
those delicious moans, hear you moaning ...
is more than wonderful. Your body ... what a beautiful
thing
is the way I like. It is wonderful to know that
you are mine, feel the pleasure that you have when lie to
me.
Ah .. I cannot forget this wonderful body
you have passion and when I'm going down
walking my tongue hot and wet for you
playing, pausing here and there as if hunting something
and then be able to witness all your masculinity there,
just for me, love. I suck you with so heartily
with much pleasure ... Well it is when we fit
at the same movement until we enjoy together.
Love ... is all so beautiful when I'm with you ..
You are just .... Wonderful!

Come

Come ... I need to hold you with all the strength of my being as

if it were the first, the only, the last time

Need cuddling your face gently and faint navigate these eyes that

lurk me with tenderness! No longer stand the appeals of

your tempting mouth.

I want you to steal a kiss, at first gently, but in this

kiss wanna feel voice of command and to faint only foreseeing the

enjoyment of other sweeping caress.

Come! And bring with you the two halves, the human half and

the beast half.

Kicks off me from my insulation, roll with me for

unknown precipices. Come!

Night

That procreate in me the holy hell

That are born and they die to make live

my locked desires ...

Because the night, lady of lust, bring with her the

miss of your smell, of your body, from your tempting mouth moist,

avid kisses ...

Your tongue restless pervades my inmost

Devour my flesh, invades my soul

Slide your fingers on my skin

Brand in verses our history

My body is your plank, my blood your ink, my desire

your slave, your pleasure ... My biggest trophy ...

Tonight

Tonight I will drink of you, enjoy all your nectar, play
in your smile, navigate through your chest, draw by your
fingers.

Tonight I will prove you, sliding the tongue by the body ,
bite your ear with pleasure, sucking your neck without
scoring, licking your treasure with caring

Tonight I will smell your scent of perfume, your warmth
when you takes your sweat, when make love, your sap,
when you get

Tonight I will love you falling in the desire of bodies
sweating in the our world until the madness of not more
satiating the love of this passion

Tonight I will be yours ... and yet without touching you ...

Lover Souls

Travelers

fellow loners

in a game of intimacies.

Only lovers,

but the desire is peaceful,

is safe, is matched.

Is the epidermis creepy,

is the mouth feeling

the flavor of freedom.

Are dilated pupils,

Are expanded nostrils

and ears alert.

The muscles go from voltage

to relaxation lazy.

Impulses in the body

the more intimate encounter of souls.

The face is relaxed,

the smile is easy

and carefree.

Abandonment of preoccupation

of want something,

since everything has ...

The spirits withdraw from their bodies,

have fun with the free energies.

Calm impulsive hearts,

soothe the anxieties

of minds to such an extent

that human limitations

be abandoned,

so that the natural mating

of the bodies are found

integrated into the whole.

If ever looks to the side and not seeing anyone

You can be sure that somewhere I'll be thinking of you.
If scrolling through the roads looking to meet you
And you find yourself undone in the dark
You can be assured that you will always be in my thoughts perfectly.

You may fight, you may even cry, but know that in my dreams...
You'll always be.
If you see the sunset, and imagine that as the day ended, so the world has abandoned you...
Be sure that in my world you will always be.

More Than Love

You are the most beautiful sunrise

You paint a smile on my face when I meet you

You are in Me, as the rain soaking me

In world has changed from the moment I met you

We are body and soul, a few drops of water

You and I, more than love

We are night and moon, as the foam and sea

You and I, more than love

Look into my eyes, heart

Tell me that our love is not a dream

This is more than love

So kiss me slowly through the darkness

I want to melt in your arms this loneliness

Put your hand in mine and see

That the sun always goes away

More than love

It is our world

Too much love

I love you my love

I Love You, We Are Love

I Love You

All the world is love

Printed in Great Britain
by Amazon

45712722R00088